HISTORIC
COMMUNITIES

Classroom Games

Bobbie Kalman & Heather Levigne

Crabtree Publishing Company

www.crabtreebooks.com

HISTORIC
COMMUNITIES

Created by Bobbie Kalman

For Melissa,
who taught me
the meaning of true friendship

Editor-in-Chief
Bobbie Kalman

Writing team
Bobbie Kalman
Heather Levigne

Managing editor
Lynda Hale

Editors
John Crossingham
Hannelore Sotzek
Amanda Bishop

Computer design
Lynda Hale

Production coordinator
Hannelore Sotzek

Printer
Worzalla Publishing Company

Special thanks to
Black Creek Pioneer Village/TRCA, Leah Kingston and her class, Kathryn Docherty

Photographs
Marc Crabtree: page 27; Bobbie Kalman at Black Creek Pioneer Village: pages 5, 10, 15; other images by Digital Stock and Eyewire, Inc.

Illustrations, colorizations, and reproductions
Barbara Bedell: front cover, title page (blocks), bee borders, pages 3 (all except slate, inkwell, and hornbook), 7, 12, 13 (top), 14 (top), 16 (bees), 17, 24, 24-25 (border), 26, 28 (holly and bells), 29 (candle and gifts); Antoinette "Cookie" Bortolon: pages 3 (inkwell and hornbook), 30 (top); Andy Cienik: pages 5, 27; Tammy Everts: pages 3 (slate), 4; John Mantha: back cover; Cecilia Ohm-Ericksen: page 28 (menorah); Sarah Pallek: page 25 (top); Margaret Amy Reiach: page 8; Bonna Rouse: title page, pages 6, 9, 14 (bottom), 19, 20, 22-23; other images by Eyewire, Inc.

Digital Prepress
Best Graphics Int'l Co.; Embassy Graphics (cover)

Crabtree Publishing Company

www.crabtreebooks.com   1-800-387-7650

PMB 16A	612 Welland Ave.	73 Lime Walk
350 Fifth Ave.,	St. Catharines,	Headington
Suite 3308	Ontario,	Oxford
New York, NY	Canada	0X3 7AD
10118	L2M 5V6	United Kingdom

Cataloging-in-Publication Data
Kalman, Bobbie
    Classroom games

p. cm. — (Historic communities)
Includes index.

ISBN 0-86505-440-1 (library bound) — ISBN 0-86505-470-3 (pbk.)
This book examines classroom games for different subjects, including mathematics, spelling, geography, and history, as well as art and music, played by children in 19th century North America.

1. Educational games—North America—History—19th century—Juvenile literature. 2. Activity programs in education—North America—History—19th century—Juvenile literature. [1. Educational games—History—19th century. 2. Games—History—19th century. 3. Schools—Exercises and recreation—History—19th century.] I. Levigne, Heather. II. Title. III. Series: Kalman, Bobbie. Historic communities.

LB1029.G3 K33 2001   j371.33'7'097—dc21   LC00-057072
                                                                                    CIP

Contents

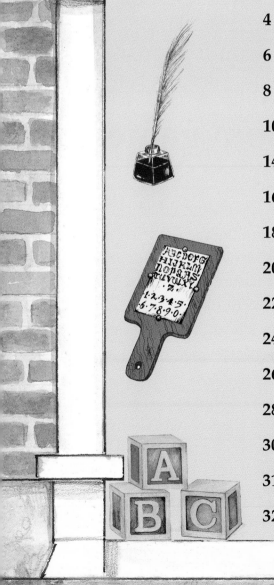

Classroom games

A hundred years ago, children did not attend large schools with many classrooms. Instead, they learned their lessons in one-room schools. In a one-room school, children of all ages studied together in a single classroom. Teachers divided the students into groups according to grade. Some teachers taught as many as eight grades in one classroom!

The three Rs

The most important subjects settler children studied in school were the three Rs: reading, 'riting, and 'rithmetic, or writing and arithmetic. Students also studied geography, history, science, and art. Most children enjoyed going to school because it gave them a break from their everyday chores.

In early schools, children did not have paper, pencils, or notebooks, as students do today. Settler children wrote their lessons on slates using a slate pencil.

Fun in the classroom

In one-room schools, many teachers often had limited supplies with which to teach the students. They had to be creative with the resources they had. To encourage children to work hard and learn their lessons, teachers often used classroom games to help make learning fun. Some games were variations of games the settlers played at home to amuse themselves in the evening.

Learning to behave

Many of the lessons settler children learned included instructions on morals and values. The books they read in school taught them to be honest, obedient, and kind toward others. In some schools, children studied the Bible. They memorized passages and recited them aloud in front of the class.

The teacher is showing that her students are the "apples of her eyes," which means she likes them a lot!

5

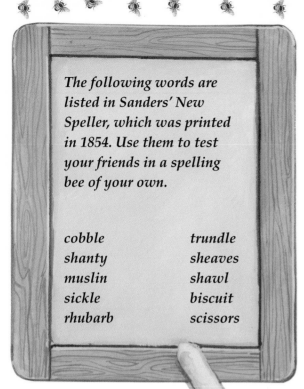

The following words are listed in Sanders' New Speller, which was printed in 1854. Use them to test your friends in a spelling bee of your own.

cobble	*trundle*
shanty	*sheaves*
muslin	*shawl*
sickle	*biscuit*
rhubarb	*scissors*

Spelling bees

Spelling was one of the most important subjects settler children studied. Good spelling skills helped children become better readers, and reading was necessary to perform jobs such as shopkeeping and teaching.

Spelling bees

Spelling bees were popular classroom games in settler times. Children enjoyed competing against one another to see who was the best speller in the class. Teachers still use spelling bees today to test their students' spelling skills. To play, the teacher divides the students into two teams. The teams line up on opposite sides of the classroom. One by one, the students are given a word to spell. When they spell a word correctly, they earn a point for their team. If they do not spell the word correctly, they are out of the game and must return to their seat. The teacher continues giving words to spell until only one student remains standing.

I spy with my little eye...

There are several versions of a children's game called I Spy. For this version of I Spy, the students are divided into two teams. To start the game, one person says, "I spy, with my little eye, something that begins with the letter ___." A person on the opposing team must locate the item that begins with that letter and then spell its name correctly. Teams receive one point for each correct answer. When each student has given a word to another player to spell and has also spelled a word himself or herself, the points are tallied. The team with the most points wins the game.

Play a game of I Spy using the picture on the opposite page. You can play alone or with your classmates. "I spy, with my little eye, something that begins with the letter..."

1. W	*6. L*
2. P	*7. F*
3. S	*8. T*
4. G	*9. B*
5. O	*10. H*

7

Alphabet games

Settler children played alphabet games to improve their **vocabulary** and reading skills. Alphabet games are also known as **word chains**.

I Love My Love

In this old-fashioned word game, players choose a letter of the alphabet and list a person's name, the place in which he or she lives, and a personality trait. For example, for the letter S, a player might say, "I love my love with an S because his name is Steven, he lives in Scotland, and he is smart."

The Preacher's Cat

The Preacher's Cat is similar to I Love My Love, but the rhyme is different. The first player starts the game with the letter A. He or she might say, "The preacher's cat is an angry cat, and her name is Abigail." The next person has to use words beginning with the letter B to describe the cat's personality and its name.

(above) Steven is a smart Scottish son—his songs sound simply superb!

(right) Abigail's attitude is awful! She is always angry.

Initials

This game is played by two people. One person asks the other a series of questions. The other person must answer the questions using the letters of his or her initials. For example, a girl named Lucy Grant would use words that start with the letters L and G to answer the questions. Answer the questions below using your own initials.

1. What is your name?
2. What do you like to eat?
3. What do you study in school?
4. Which are your favorite colors?
5. Which are some of your favorite animals?

Lucy Grant likes lavender and green. Her favorite animals are lynxes and geese. She snacks on lollipops and gingerbread, and her best school subjects are literature and geography!

9

*Children **parsed** sentences, or explained the meaning and function of each word.*

Word games

Settler children used word games to increase their vocabulary and help them think quickly. Often it is easier to understand and remember a word if you can first use it in a fun way and then repeat it in different ways.

Crambo

The name of this game comes from the Greek word for cabbage, but no one knows why this game is named after a vegetable! Crambo is also known as I'm Thinking of a Word. The object of the game is to guess a mystery word. One person says, "I'm thinking of a word that rhymes with ___." The other players take turns asking questions to help them guess the word.

Here is an example of Crambo. Try playing this game with your friends.

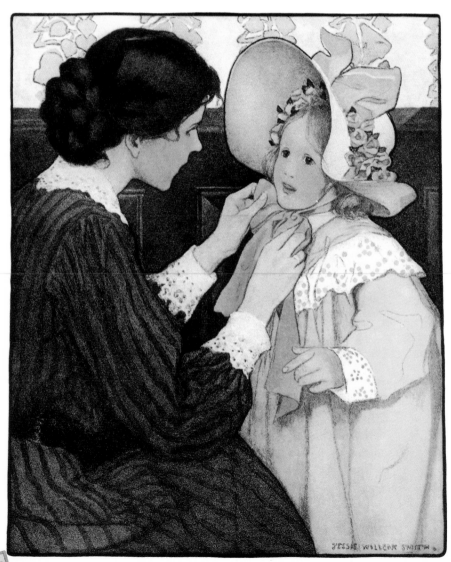

"I'm thinking of a word that rhymes with fat."
"Is it on the floor beneath your feet?"
"No, it isn't a mat."
"Is it a child who misbehaves?"
"No, it isn't a brat."
"Is it a rodent?"
"No, it isn't a rat."
"Is it a furry pet that chases mice?"
"No, it isn't a cat."
"Is it something to wear on your head?"
"Yes, it's a hat!"

Rebus

A **rebus** is a type of word game that combines pictures with letters to create words and sentences. For example, a picture of an eye, then the letter A, a picture of a door, followed by the letter U creates the phrase, "I adore you." Create your own rebus puzzles, such as the one above, to test your friends and classmates.

Sentence Relay

For a sentence relay, divide the classroom into two teams. Each player takes a turn writing one word on the blackboard. To make the game more difficult, the teacher can tell each player the type of word he or she must write, such as a **noun**, **verb**, **adverb**, or **adjective**. The first team that completes a sentence wins the relay.

Anagrams

Children played Anagrams to improve their spelling skills. They wrote the letters of the alphabet on squares of paper and turned the squares face down on a desk. You can play Anagrams with the tiles from a Scrabble® game.

To start the game, each player chooses a square and turns it over. Players take turns turning over squares until someone is able to use the letters to make a word. Then s/he calls out the word and takes the letters in the word. Each person continues turning over letters, and new words are made. Players can take whole words from other players if they can use all the letters to make new words.

The word "anagram" comes from a Greek word that means "to write anew." In some versions of Anagrams, players simply scramble the letters of a word to make a new word.

Rigamarole

Rigamarole is a tongue-twisting memory game. It is best played in a group of three to six players. Players make up **alliterative** phrases using the first letters of numbers. Each player must remember the phrases and repeat them before giving his or her own phrase. To begin, the first person makes up a phrase using words that begin with O, such as "One orange octopus." The next person repeats the first phrase and then creates a phrase for the number two using the letter T, such as "Two tiny thimbles." Can you think of a phrase for the number three and the letter T?

Four festive female friends fail to find fun frolicking in fascinating fall foliage.

Creative writing

Writing stories and poetry helped children practice their language skills. They wrote their lessons in books filled with unlined paper and used **copybooks** to practice their **penmanship**, or handwriting skills. Copybooks contained samples of letters and words to copy in a person's best handwriting.

Journals

Pioneer students wrote in copybooks or on slates, but you can keep your creative writing in a journal. Write down all the things you see, hear, smell, taste, and touch in your schoolyard or backyard. Then write a paragraph about all these things. Using all your senses to describe your surroundings will help you become a better writer.

At recess, Molly picked a bouquet of fragrant flowers and nibbled on wild berries. She was careful not to touch a prickly patch of thistles growing nearby. She heard a robin singing and saw a gopher scurrying into its hole.

Fun with adjectives

An adjective is a word such as "warm" that describes a person, place, or thing. For this game, each student writes down nine adjectives, which are inserted into a story. The students are not allowed to read the story before choosing their adjectives, so the words are seldom appropriate. The story can be very funny, especially if the names of the people in the story are those of their classmates!

On a sheet of paper, write nine adjectives. Put them into the story below or write your own story and ask a friend to choose adjectives for it. Please do not write in this book!

On a ___ day in June, (girl's name) and (boy's name) went to the nearby swimming hole. The sun was ___, and the water was ___ and ___. The children brought their ___ dog Sandy along with them. As they skipped down the path, they sang ___ songs. Suddenly, Sandy saw a ___ rabbit bounding through the ___ bushes and began barking. He ran after the ___ rabbit, and SPLASH, Sandy fell into the swimming hole! (boy's name) and (girl's name) laughed at the sight of their ___ dog.

All about adverbs

Adverbs are words that modify verbs, or action words. Use five adverbs to talk about what you think is happening in the picture on the right (see page 32).

The water is running ____.
The leaves are rustling ____.
The sun is shining ____.
The boy is walking ____.
The girl is standing ____.

Students were asked to read information out loud and to recite poems and stories in front of the class.

Why do you think these children are looking in the stream? What might they have lost in the water?

15

Try playing Buzz with the number three—it is very tricky!

1	2	3	6
4	5	6	15
7	8	9	24
12	15	18	

Arithmetic

When settler children grew older, many of the jobs they had to do required good arithmetic skills. For example, farmers needed to know basic math such as addition, subtraction, division, and multiplication in order to get a fair price for their crops and livestock. Arithmetic also helped dressmakers calculate the amount of fabric needed to make clothing. Storekeepers used it to keep track of the **barters**, or trades, they made with the settlers.

Buzzzzzz!

The game of Buzz helped settler children practice their multiplication tables. To play, students sit in a circle and begin to count in turn. Whenever a player comes to the number seven, a multiple of seven, or a number with a seven in it, he or she has to say "buzz" instead of the number. If the player forgets to say "buzz" at the right time, he or she is out of the game. The rest of the players continue to count until only one person is left. The higher the players count, the harder it is to remember when to say "buzz!"

No problem!

Arithmetic puzzles helped settler children improve their problem-solving skills. You can test your math skills with a game called Nine Digits. To play, cut nine small squares of paper. Number each square from one to nine. Arrange the numbers in three rows (as shown in the diagram) so that when they are added across, up and down, or diagonally, they always add up to fifteen. For the answers to this game, turn to page 32.

Multiplication or Division Relay

In this math game, students try to solve problems as quickly as possible. The teacher writes multiplication or division problems on cards. Each row of students makes up a team. When the teacher says, "Ready, set, multiply (or divide)!" the first person in each row takes a card and goes up to the blackboard. The students solve the questions as fast as they can and then return to their seat. Then the next person in the row goes up to the blackboard to solve a problem. Each student must solve his or her problem before the next person can take a turn. The first team to solve all the problems and sit down wins the game.

Fun with fractions

A **fraction** is a smaller part of a whole object or number. To help understand fractions, look at the sandwich. It is cut into four pieces. Each piece is one-fourth of the whole sandwich. Now look at the pizza. Into how many fractions is it divided? If you eat one fraction of the pizza, how many are left?

This girl is solving a division problem. Figure out the answer and check page 32.

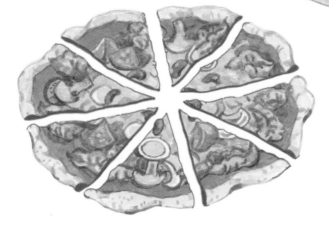

Food fractions are fun to figure out! You can also learn about fractions using coins. For example, one dollar is made up of four quarters. If you spend two quarters, you have one-half of the dollar left. What fraction would you have left if you spent three quarters?

17

Geography

In geography class, students memorized the names of countries, capital cities, lakes, rivers, and mountains. To help students learn about places around the world, some teachers had a spinning globe in the classroom. Settler children dreamed of visiting places they learned about in geography class.

Alphabet Geography

Students played this geography game using the globe in their classroom. To play, one person names a place that begins with the letter A, such as Africa. The next person must think of a place that begins with the last letter of Africa, which is also A. If the second player says "Albuquerque," the third player must name a place that starts with E, such as England. If a player cannot think of a word, s/he is out of the game. Players continue until only one person is left.

Same game, different rules!

You can play a different version of Alphabet Geography by naming cities and countries in alphabetical order. For example, the first player names a place that begins with A, such as Australia. Now the second player thinks of a place that starts with B, such as Boston. Thinking of places that begin with X, Y, and Z is difficult, so players can agree to skip these letters when there are no words left for them. Make up some of your own Alphabet Geography games.

Each of the pictures on these two pages shows a famous landmark. Identify the landmarks and the countries in which they are located. (Here is a hint to help you get started—the pictures are numbered from one to four, and they are in alphabetical order.) Turn to page 32 to find out if your answers are correct.

Souvenirs

For this geography game, the teacher puts the names of several cities or countries from around the world into a hat or basket. Each student picks a location from the hat and makes a list of the things he or she might bring back as souvenirs after a trip to that place. Then the student reads the list of items to the class. The other students must guess the location based on the types of souvenirs.

In which country would you find a sombrero, serape, piñata, and set of maracas? The answer is on page 32. Make up your own list of souvenirs from a country and try to stump your friends!

History

I am a queen who won the Egyptian throne from my brother and was friends with Julius Caesar. Who am I?

Settler children learned about significant people, places, and events in history. The people shown on this page are all historic figures.

Who Am I?

For this game, one person thinks of a famous historical person, such as a president, inventor, or writer. Each of the other players must ask questions to try to guess the name of the famous person. Players can ask only questions that can be answered with "yes" or "no." If a player asks twenty questions without guessing correctly, that player is out of the game. If no one can guess the answer before asking twenty questions, the person who chose the historical figure wins the game.

I am an English playwright and poet. Some of my famous works include "Romeo and Juliet" and "Hamlet." Who am I?

I am a British monarch who ruled England from 1558 to 1603. Who am I?

I am an Italian explorer who found the Caribbean Islands while searching for India. My ships were the Niña, the Pinta, and the Santa Maria. Who am I?

For the answers to this game, turn to page 32.

Let's make a memory!

Native Americans did not record the events of their lives in books. Instead, they passed on their languages, traditions, and lessons by telling stories to their children and grandchildren. Over time, these stories changed slightly, but they were not forgotten.

Make a record of your history. Create an album using pictures of yourself at different ages. On the first page, write your full name and the year and place you were born. Use pictures that show significant events in your life, such as your first birthday, the first day of school, and those people who are important to you. Under each picture, describe the event that is taking place.

Some Native Americans recorded their history with pictures and symbols.

When my parents brought me home from the hospital after I was born, my family had a party to celebrate my arrival. My mother was so proud of me!

For my second Christmas, my grandparents came to visit. They gave me lots of gifts!

For my fifth birthday, my parents gave me a new two-wheeled bicycle. While I was riding it, I fell off and broke my arm. All my friends signed my cast!

Outdoor classrooms

Sometimes, teachers took their students outside to learn from nature. They observed animals and, as part of their science class, they learned about different plants and how to grow them.

School gardens

A school garden taught settler children about living things. The students planted seeds and tended the crops that grew. In the fall, they felt that their hard work was rewarded when they were able to harvest vegetables and fruits from the garden. School gardens helped the rest of the pioneers as well. Some of the food grown in school gardens was distributed to families who did not have gardens of their own.

Children worked hard at planting a garden in the schoolyard. They enjoyed growing a variety of fruits, vegetables, and flowers. They especially loved eating the "fruits of their labor."

Let's go on a scavenger hunt!

In a scavenger hunt, children search for objects that are hidden in a certain area. Using the picture above, find the items on the list below.

* hornet's nest
* garter snake
* scarecrow
* spiderweb
* gopher
* sunflowers
* rabbit

* butterfly
* pumpkin
* bird's nest
* compost
* strawberry plant
* shovel
* bumblebee

Create your own scavenger hunt! Make a list of things in your schoolyard or backyard and have your friends hunt for them. The first person to find all the items wins the game.

23

Art

Art classes were very important to settler children because they taught them how to paint pictures. Art class also gave them the opportunity to create beautiful crafts that they could enjoy at home as well as at school.

Dolls

Dolls were favorite toys of many pioneer girls, but most families could not afford to buy porcelain dolls with silk dresses. Instead, girls made their own dolls out of yarn and handkerchiefs. Other dolls were made of dried cornhusks.

Nature's artwork

Settler children gathered and preserved natural materials such as nuts, pine cones, leaves, flowers, seeds, and berries to make decorative items such as wreaths. They hung flowers and herbs upside down from the rafters of the roof until the plants were dry. Children also pressed flowers between heavy books to preserve them. Some plants and berries were used to make dyes for fabric and yarn.

Create a nature game

Make a nature board game you can play with your friends. Cut a piece of cardboard fifteen inches (38 cm) square. Use a pencil to mark the board with one-inch (2.5 cm) squares. Write instructions about nature on each square, such as "You spotted a barn owl—move ahead two spaces." Make sure some squares cause you to move backward as well, such as "You forgot to water your garden." Use pine cones, acorns, or small stones as playing pieces.

Thaumatrope

A thaumatrope was a favorite settler toy. Each side of the thaumatrope had a picture. When the strings on either side of the pictures were twisted and released, the thaumatrope spun around, making the two pictures appear to be a single image. Follow these directions to make your own version of this pioneer game.

4. Wind up the strings. When you release the strings, your thaumatrope will spin and form one picture.

1. Cut a circle from a piece of cardboard.

2. Punch two holes on opposite sides of the circle and tie a piece of string through each one.

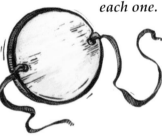

3. Draw a picture on each side of the circle. You can draw a fish on one side and waves on the other, as shown here, or make up your own pictures.

People love to look at art because they see different things in pictures. What do you see happening in this picture? How does it make you feel? Ask a friend to look at the picture and share his or her feelings with you.

Handmade crafts

From an early age, settler children learned how to make handicrafts. One way to practice these skills was to devote part of the school day to **domestic arts** such as woodworking and sewing. The skills learned at a young age were also useful when children became adults. Many people earned a living by making handmade items such as clothing, furniture, and textiles.

Sewing and embroidery

Girls learned to sew as soon as they were old enough to hold a needle and thread. They first learned how to sew simple designs such as patchwork or cross-stitched **samplers**. As they became more advanced, they sewed clothes for their dolls, and eventually they made their own clothes as well. In pioneer days, **patterns** were not always available, so girls carefully took apart old dresses to use as patterns for new ones. Sewing machines were not used until 1851, so the ability to make small, neat stitches was an important skill. Girls who had good sewing skills often grew up to be seamstresses.

Working with wood

Boys learned how to **whittle**, or carve, at a young age. They made simple wooden objects such as **whirligigs** and whistles. As they grew older, they worked on more difficult projects and made objects for the home, including bowls and stools. Good carpentry skills helped prepare boys for the task of building a home after they grew up and got married.

Classroom quilt

After they made clothing, the pioneers sewed quilts from the leftover scraps of fabric. Children learned how to make small patchwork quilts at a young age. You can also make a quilt with your classmates. Each person stitches his or her initials onto a piece of fabric that is about five inches (12.5 cm) square. Add symbols such as flowers, hearts, or stars to your initials or make up your own design. When all the squares are stitched, ask your teacher or another adult to sew them together into one large sheet. Use this piece as the top of your quilt. Cut a large sheet the same size as the top part of the quilt to use as the back and fill the quilt with cotton batting.

*When people get together to make a quilt, the event is called a **quilting** bee.*

You can make a picture quilt to show a scene such as this one.

Holiday games

The settlers lived in small close-knit communities. Most of the people who lived in town knew one another by name. Everyone participated in community events such as social gatherings, meetings, and celebrations. These events often took place in the schoolhouse. On holidays such as Christmas, Halloween, and Thanksgiving, the pioneers held dances, prayer meetings, parties, and pageants in the one-room school.

The holiday game

On these two pages are symbols of some of the holidays celebrated by the settlers. Find the symbols that go with each holiday. Some of the symbols apply to more than one!

Identify the following symbols:
- five Christmas
- two New Year
- three Thanksgiving
- two Halloween
- one St. Patrick's Day
- two Hanukkah
- three Easter

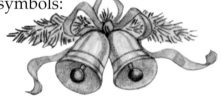

See page 32 for the answers to this game.

A candle is lit on each night of this December holiday.

On this "green" holiday, settlers of Irish descent remembered a favorite saint by eating green food, drinking beverages that had been dyed green, and parading around the streets in green costumes.

Beware of black cats and scary jack-o'-lanterns on this frightful night!

A cornucopia represents fruits of the harvest on this holiday.

At the stroke of midnight, bells ring, people sing, wishes are made, and something new is born. What is this holiday?

The settlers placed candles on a tree to decorate it for this favorite winter holiday.

This bird makes a fine dinner for two special days of the year. What are they?

This holiday has three famous symbols. What are the symbols and which is the holiday?

Gifts are given throughout the year, but there are two special reasons for gift-giving here!

Making music

Music was a main source of entertainment for the settlers. At school, rhymes and songs were often used to teach children about everyday life and culture. Many songs taught children about life, marriage, work, friendship, and even historical events. For example, the song "Quaker, How Art Thee?" teaches the importance of being a good neighbor.

Making music

Some children learned how to play musical instruments at home, and they shared their musical talents with their classmates. Fiddles, harmonicas, and guitars were some examples of instruments played by the settlers. Few families had large, expensive items such as pianos or harpsichords. Some children were lucky enough to take music lessons at a music school or from a traveling music teacher.

Look at the musical instruments on this page and answer the questions beside them.

Which musical instrument is associated with the sound of angel music?

This violin is for classical music. Which type is used for a barn dance?

These two "pianos" were favorites with the settlers.

Which is the zeze, and which is the harpsichord? See page 32 for all the answers.

Quaker, How Art Thee

"Quaker, How Art Thee?" is a very old song. When the settlers sang it, they gathered in a circle. One person begins the game by singing the first line of the following verse:

Quaker, Quaker, how art thee?
Very well, I thank thee.
How's thy neighbor next to thee?
I don't know, but I'll go see.

While asking the first question, the first player points to the player on his or her right. S/he answers with the second line of the song. Then the first player asks, "How's thy neighbor, next to thee?" The player on the right answers again, and then it becomes that person's turn to sing the rhyme and inquire about the person to his or her right. The game continues around the circle until each player has had a turn. Then the game starts again, going to the left this time.

Glossary

adjective A word used to describe a noun

adverb A word used to modify a verb

alliteration The technique of using several words that begin with the same letter in a sentence

copybook A notebook in which children practiced their handwriting

cornucopia A horn overflowing with fruits, flowers, and grains displayed as a symbol of a successful harvest

domestic art Arts and crafts designed for household use

harpsichord A musical instrument similar to a piano

noun A person, place, or thing

pageant A play or skit, which tells a story and is performed for an audience

parsing The act of identifying each part of a sentence, such as nouns, verbs, and adjectives

pattern A model, such as an old piece of clothing used to cut out fabric for making new clothing

prayer meeting An event at which people gather for prayer and worship

quilting bee A social gathering at which women sew a quilt

rebus A puzzle in which pictures are used to represent words or parts of words

sampler A piece of cloth embroidered with different stitches for the purpose of practicing sewing skills

slate A thin, smooth piece of dark rock upon which children wrote

textile A cloth made from weaving or knitting

thaumatrope A two-sided toy, each side having pictures that, when the toy is spun, appear together as a single picture

verb A word used to describe an action

vocabulary The number of words known by a particular person

whirligig A spinning toy made from a length of string threaded through a hole in a round piece of wood

word chain A word game in which players test their spelling and vocabulary skills

zeze A hand-held musical instrument with metal keys that are played with the thumbs

Index

Answers

Page 6:
1. women at the well
2. pigs in a pen
3. scarecrow
4. gaggle of geese
5. oxen
6. log home
7. fence
8. trees
9. bridge
10. horses

Page 15:
The words in bold are examples of adverbs:
The water is running **slowly**.
The leaves are rustling **softly**.
The sun is shining **brightly**.
The boy is walking **carefully**.
The girl is standing **still**.

Page 16:

6	7	2
1	5	9
8	3	4

Page 17: one-quarter (¼)

Page 18:
1. Egypt (pyramids)
2. France (Eiffel Tower)
3. Greece (Parthenon)
4. Holland (windmills)

Page 19: Mexico

Page 20:
(in counterclockwise order) Cleopatra, William Shakespeare, Queen Elizabeth I, Christopher Columbus

Page 28:
Christmas: holly, bells, candles, turkey, gifts
New Year: bells sounded at midnight, a new year's baby
Thanksgiving: cornucopia, corn, turkey
Halloween: pumpkin, black cat
St. Patrick's Day: four-leaf clover
Hanukkah: Menorah, gifts
Easter: colored eggs, lilies, bunny

Page 30:
The harp is associated with angel music. A fiddle is a type of violin used for a barn dance. The harpsichord is on the left, and the zeze is on the right.

1 2 3 4 5 6 7 8 9 0 Printed in U.S.A. 9 8 7 6 5 4 3 2 1 0